CAPTIONS:

☼ *Cover:* Sunset over the dunes at Island Beach
State Park

☼ *Front endpaper:* Shells cover the beach in
Barnegat Light, Long Beach Island.

☼ *Page 1:* A sunny day on the beach at Avalon cre-
ates a classic beach tableau.

☼ *Pages 2–3:* Evening action draws visitors to the
boardwalk at Seaside Heights.

☼ *Pages 4–5:* A lone fisherman stands sentinel in
the surf at Stone Harbor.

☼ *Pages 6–7:* Late afternoon light bathes the Great
Sound near Stone Harbor.

☼ *Table of Contents:* A couple make their way past
Cape May Point Lighthouse in the fading evening light.

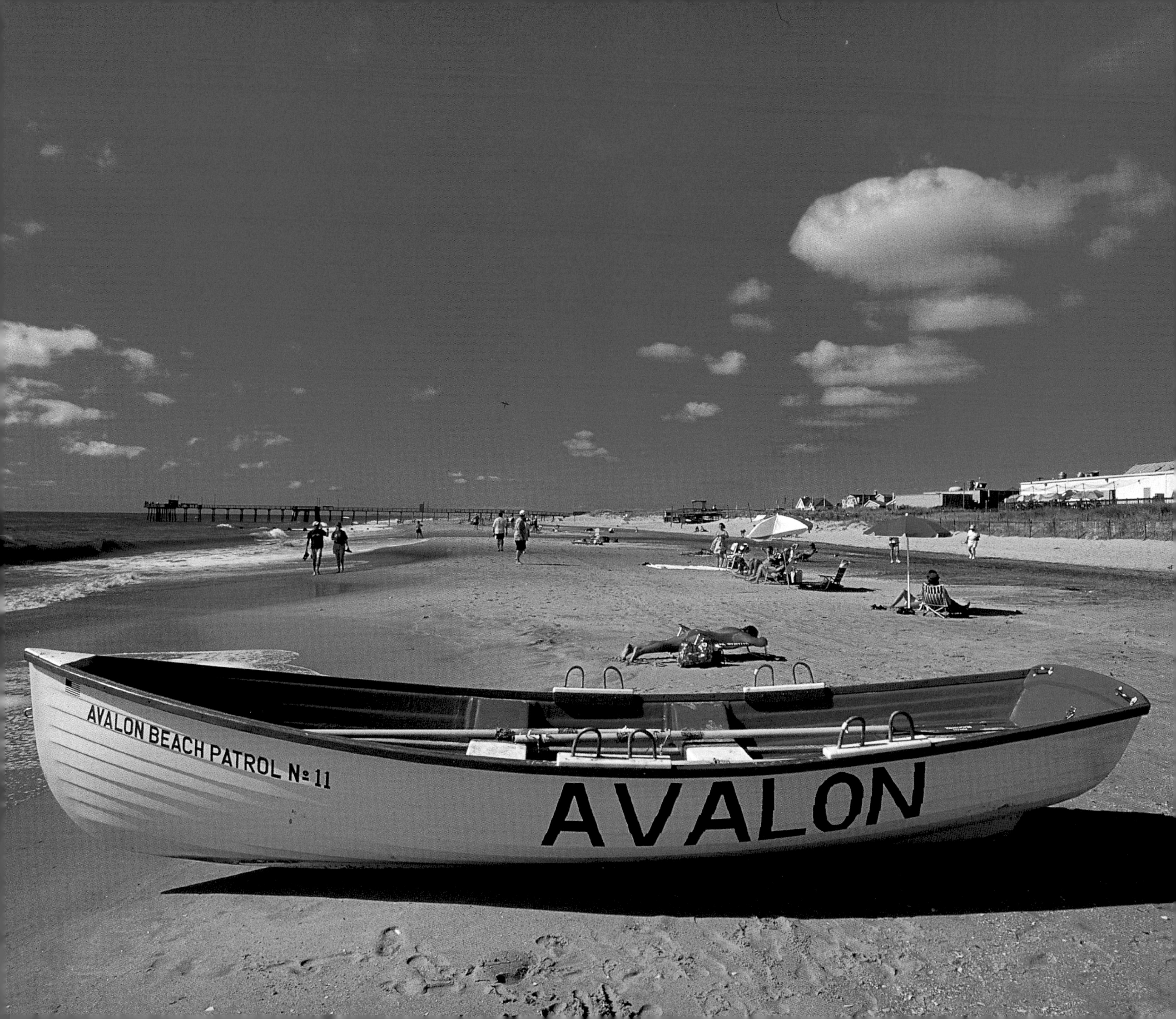
AVALON BEACH PATROL № 11
AVALON

Acknowledgments

To my parents, Joyce and Kris.

I've been photographing at the Shore since 1980, when *National Geographic* assigned me to shoot a story about New Jersey. In the ensuing years, several other magazines sent me back to my favorite summer spot. I'd like to thank Bob Gilka, then director of photography at *National Geographic,* Albert Chiang of *Islands* magazine, Bill Black, then of *Travel & Leisure,* and Dan Westergren of *National Geographic Traveler* magazine for giving me an opportunity to hang out at the beach with my camera.

Among the many folks who have helped me along the way are Carol and George Hryvniak, who always made a place for me in a succession of beach rentals over the years, Lt. Mike DaPonte of the U.S. Coast Guard; Mike Fritz, Joe Darlington, Jack Morey; "Doc" Daugenbaugh, a superb helicopter pilot; Shriver's Candy, Lisa Whitley of Fralingers, the PR departments of every major Atlantic City casino, Tom and Sue Carroll of the Mainstay Inn; The Abbey, Caroline at The Stone Pony, The Ocean Grove Camp Meeting Association, and Michael Fee (aka "The Maestro").

My thanks go to Andrew Hudson, Chuck O'Rear, Ian Lloyd, great photographers and sage advisors; Jenny Barry, Ed Faherty, and my brother Gary Krist, who kindly took time to shape up my prose. As always, my thanks and love go to my wife Peggy and my sons Matt, Brian, and Jon, beach boys all. —*Bob Krist*

The author and his parents in Ortley Beach, 1954.

Down the Shore

Bob Krist

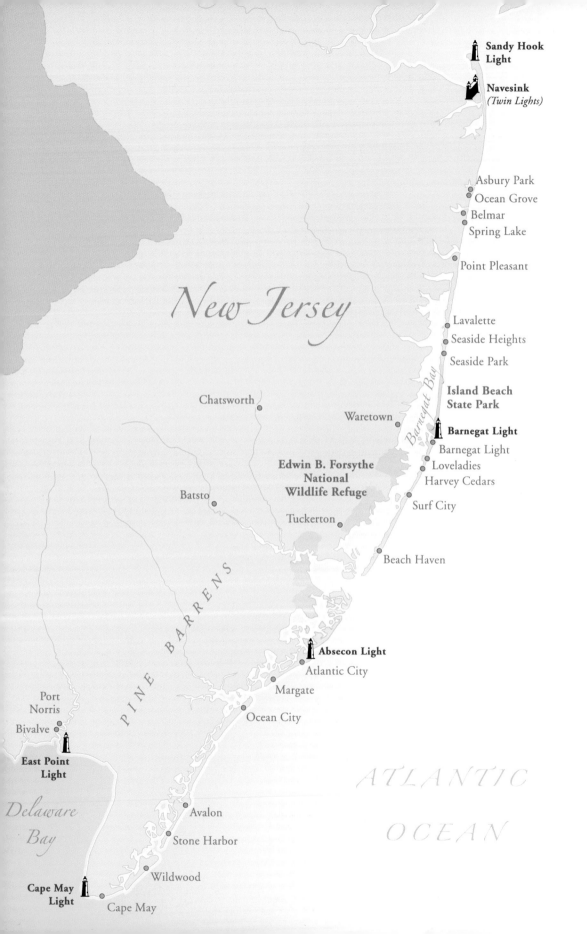

Published by:
Old Mill Productions
New Hope, PA
www.bobkrist.com

In conjunction with:
Photo Tour Books, Inc.
San Diego, CA
www.phototourbooks.com

Distributed to the trade by:
NBN (National Book Network)
Lanham, MD
800-462-6420
www.nbnbooks.com

ISBN: 1-930495-48-X (cl.)

First edition, May 2005.

Photo of Bruce Springsteen on page 30 © Corbis.

Photographs and text by Bob Krist © 2005. All rights reserved. Designed by Andrew Hudson. Map by Ed Faherty of Faherty Design. Printed in Korea.

For stock photography requests, contact Bob Krist at 215-862-4828 or bobkrist@aol.com

These books make great welcome gifts and corporate amenities. Ask about customized covers with large orders. For quantity discounts, call Peggy Krist at 215-862-4828.

Contents

Introduction

I'm standing in the predawn darkness, waiting for sunrise with my tripod jammed in the sand, when the night breezes go calm. The sun edges over the Atlantic's rim and reveals a tableau of incredible beauty—grass-covered dunes, wide, empty beaches as far as the eye can see and an oceanscape that stretches to the horizon. It's hardly a scene one expects to see in the most densely populated state in the country.

But this is Island Beach State Park, one of the last stretches of pristine beach on the Eastern seaboard. It's as much a part of the Jersey Shore as the boardwalks, motels, and amusement piers that comprise the more common view of this 127-mile-long stretch of coastline. Smack in the heart of the Northeastern megalopolis, with one third of the population of the United States within a day's drive, it serves as all things to all people, not to mention millions of migrating birds and other wildlife.

Like many good things, the shore is threatened: by over-development, pollution, and the forces of nature. But this is New Jersey, the place that wrote the book on toughness and resilience. And so, at least for the time being, its seacoast manages to survive, and even thrive.

So join me on this visual trip "down the shore." Whether you crave the honky-tonk boardwalk atmosphere—redolent of pine tar, caramel popcorn, and grilling sausage—or a pristine beach to solitarily commune with shorebirds and sea breezes, or the glitzy elegance of a casino penthouse, you'll find it in these pages. From the sublime to ridiculous, it's all good, and it's all pure 'Jersey.

12

☀ A couple on the beach at Cape May greets the rising sun.

On the Boardwalk

Necessity is often the mother of invention. The very first boardwalk in the nation came into being in New Jersey to solve a simple but vexing problem: people tracking sand all over hotels when they came back from a day at the beach. Although certain accounts mention something called a "flirtation walk" in Cape May as early as 1868, it was in 1870 that Atlantic City hoteliers Alexander Boardman and Jacob Keim proposed the construction of a wooden beachside walkway. The city council agreed, and by June of that year the Boardwalk opened with ceremonies and parades.

Other beach resorts took notice. Soon towns like Asbury Park, Ocean City, Seaside Heights, Point Pleasant and Wildwood followed suit, and boardwalks became a staple up and down the Jersey coast.

Always on the cutting edge, the Atlantic City Boardwalk developed other attractions for the amusement of its visitors. Graceful wicker chairs appeared around 1880, and a few years later came amusement piers like the famous Steel Pier, whose legendary High-Diving Horse would plunge sixty feet from a high platform into a pool.

Although casino gambling revitalized the town in the early 1970's, arguably the grandest Boardwalk attraction of them all is still the Miss America Pageant. It too was born of necessity: the necessity to stretch the tourist season after Labor Day. In September 1921, local businessmen and hoteliers organized a parade and a beauty contest with only eight entrants. An immediate success, the pageant grew to become an American icon, like the Boardwalk itself.

Colorful neon illuminates the Boardwalk in Atlantic City.

🍸 *Left:* Since the advent of legalized gambling in 1978, casinos have dominated the skyline of Atlantic City.

🍸 *Above:* Miss America contestants cruise the Boardwalk in the traditional "Show Us Your Shoes" parade.

🍸 *Left:* The floor of Bally's Wild Wild West Casino is lined with slot machines. There are a dozen casinos in Atlantic City, generating billions of dollars each year.

🍸 *Above:* There are almost as many security monitors as slot machines in most casinos, ever on the lookout for card sharps and others who try to beat the system.

🍸 *Right:* The bustle on the Boardwalk goes on day and night in the Queen of Resorts.

🍸 The gold and glitz of the gaming floor at the The Hilton Resort and Casino.

The Borgata Hotel and Casino is the tallest building in New Jersey.

🍨 *Left:* Casinos love to pamper their high rollers, gamblers with deep pockets who regularly wager major money, and often treat them to penthouse rooms and white glove service.

🍨 *Above:* Don Rickles, an ageless Atlantic City favorite, clowns in his dressing room before a show. The casinos draw top entertainers from around the world to headline their shows.

🍨 *Right:* Celebrity impersonators, like these Elvis and Rod Stewart lookalikes preparing in their dressing room, are often featured in the Legends shows in Atlantic City.

🍧 *Left:* Plastic clowns and larger-than-life action figures share the boardwalk with families in Seaside Heights.

🍧 *Right:* Waterparks, like this one on the boardwalk in Ocean City, are enjoyed by kids of all ages.

🍧 *Below:* Scenes from the boardwalk in Wildwood.

🍦 Three "little miracles" in the annual Ocean City Baby Parade, a boardwalk fixture since 1909 and one of the oldest in the country.

The "Men in Black" escort their charge on the boards during the Baby Parade in Ocean City.

🍨 *Left:* A typical Saturday afternoon in Wildwood may find members of the New Jersey Elks Club gathering for their annual parade outside a Doo Wop era motel.

🍨 *Above:* "Uncle Sam" waves to the crowds from his perch on an Elks Club float.

The famous Mummers of Philadelphia also strut their stuff in Wildwood.

🍨 *Left:* "The Boss," Bruce Springsteen, a Jersey Shore legend and champion of Asbury Park's renewal struggle, performs in concert at the Convention Center.

🍨 *Above:* Springsteen got his start at the Stone Pony, which still showcases local Shore talent.

🍨 *Right:* "Tilly," the mascot of the defunct Palace Amuseuments, is an area icon.

🍨 *Above:* The majestic Essex and Sussex overlooks Spring Lake's boardwalk. 🍨 *Following:* A boardwalk pizzeria in Wildwood.

Mama Leone's II
CHICKEN
GYRO
SOUVLAKI OR GYRO ON PITA BREAD
2722

Life's A Beach

Along New Jersey's 127-mile-long coastline, there are beaches to suit nearly every taste. All of them feature sand and sea, of course, but within those parameters, there is an astonishing range of character to these strands. From the texture of the sand, to the type of surf break, to the personalities of folks who might be spreading their blanket in your vicinity, the choices abound. And those beaches also play host to a myriad of activities—kite flying, national marble tournaments, weddings, hot rod shows, and of course, sand castle contests.

Looking for kid-friendly beaches for your family? Try Long Beach Island if you like a quiet atmosphere and beaches of sugary sand. Prefer a broader beach, more firm-ly-packed sand, with a lot of amusements? Well, then Wildwood is the place to go. For surf fishermen who crave long stretches of sand all to themselves, Island Beach State Park is a favorite destination. College kids looking for sea-side fun congregate in Belmar. For some of the best surf breaks in the East, Manasquan Inlet and the Hogate Jetty are great choices.

No matter which beach you choose, chances are you won't be far from the watchful eyes of a trained lifeguard. The Jersey Shore was the home to the first-ever professional lifeguard corps in the United States, the Atlantic City Beach Patrol, established in 1891. Since that time, beach patrols have ensured the safety of millions of beach-goers.

Crowds on the beach at Seaside Heights.

✗ *Left:* On a sunny Saturday afternoon, the beach at Ocean City is packed with people.

✗ *Above:* Beach umbrellas create a colorful pattern at Avon-by-the-Sea.

✗ *Right:* Sporting an unusual hairstyle, a lifeguard keeps an eye on the beach at Barnegat Light.

✗ *Following page:* Couples stroll Spray Beach on Long Beach Island.

🏖 *Left:* A boogie boarder catches the curl at a break off the beach at Lavallette.

🏖 *Above:* A young boogie boarder uses his head to solve the problem of transporting his boards to the beach in Seaside Park.

🏖 *Right:* An aerial view of the surf near Mantaloking.

🏖 *Following pages:* Unusual and avant-garde architecture characterizes many of the beachfront homes in the towns of Harvey Cedars and Loveladies on Long Beach Island.

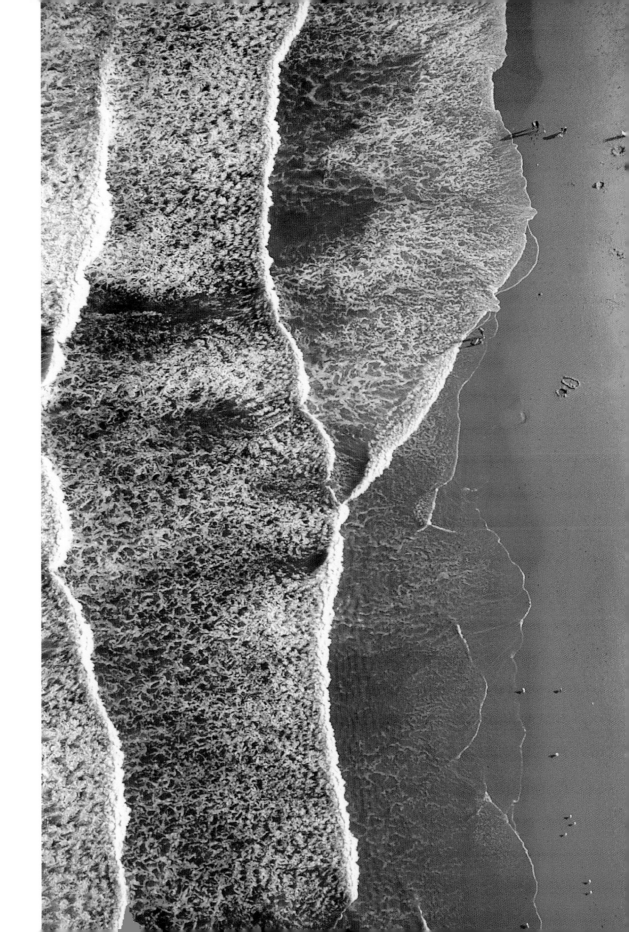

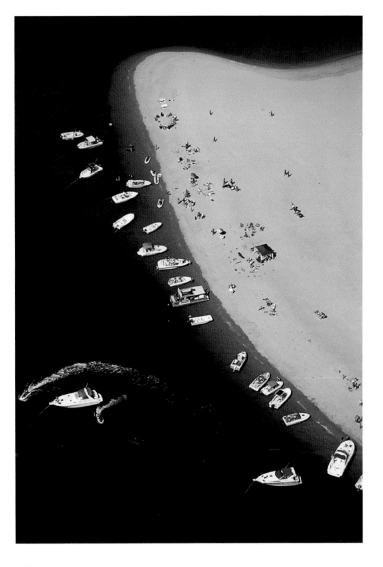

Left and above: Champagne Island is a sandy atoll in the Hereford Inlet and is popular with boaters.

🏖 *Left:* Look Ma, no hands! A youngster uses his head to obtain refreshment on the strand in Beach Haven.

🏖 *Above:* If you plan ahead you can shoot the Christmas card picture in the summer, like this Mom on the beach at Cape May.

Spending a dog-day afternoon at the beach in Cape May.

🦀 *Left:* A pair of lifeguards practice surf rescue techniques at Barnegat Light.

🦀 *Above:* Rowing races are a staple of the lifeguard tournaments held every summer up and down the Jersey Shore.

🦀 *Right:* Members of the U.S. Coast Guard practice rescue techniques in the choppy bay waters near their base in Cape May.

🦀 *Following pages:* A gusty autumn evening churns up the clouds over the dunes of Island Beach State Park.

Heritage & Traditions

To the casual observer, the Jersey Shore may appear to be merely a string of interchangeable beach and blender-drink towns, but the area boasts a rich history and heritage. Many of what have become familiar coastal features of the United States had their origins here: the oldest standing lighthouse at Sandy Hook (1764), the first boardwalk at Atlantic City (1870), and the first seashore resort at Cape May (1761), to name a few.

Much of the heritage of the Jersey Shore springs from surprising roots. Lucy the Margate Elephant, now a National Historic Site, was first constructed as a public relations gimmick to attract real estate buyers to the then-worthless sandy stretches below Atlantic City. Lively shore towns that pulse with the energy of vacationing teenagers and families, like Ocean City and Belmar, began life as staid religious retreats. Saltwater taffy was "invented" when seawater washed out a candy store. And Wildwood's neon-topped motels, once considered tacky, are now revered as embodiments of Doo Wop architecture.

Today, you can still see decoy carvers practice their craft in workshops at Tuckerton Seaport. Re-enactors at the Emlen Physick Estate, Cold Spring Village and Allaire State Park bring history to life as they interpret the past with great attention to detail in carefully restored buildings from bygone eras. You can climb the towers of 200-year-old lighthouses and the masts of the A.J. Meerwald, a circa-1928 oyster dredge that still plies the waters of the Delaware Bay. Far from being dry history, the traditions of the Jersey Shore are alive and well and waiting to be experienced.

The East Point Lighthouse on the Delaware Bay was built in 1849 and is the second oldest lighthouse in New Jersey.

Left: Sandy Hook Lighthouse is the oldest continuously operating lighthouse in the country.

It was built in 1764 in response to the pleas of New York merchants and sea captains after several disastrous shipwrecks off the coast here in 1761. The lighthouse was declared a National Historic Monument in 1964, on the two hundredth anniversary of its first lighting.

Right: The structure's aging Fresnel lens refracts the surrounding landscape. When it was built, Sandy Hook Lighthouse stood a mere 500 feet from the tip of the Hook. Today, thanks to two hundred years of sand and tide movement, it is located over 1.5 miles from the tip of the peninsula.

Left: The 1862 Twin Lights of Navesink offer views of Sandy Hook and even the southern tip of Manhattan.

Above: Barnegat Light, on the northern tip of Long Beach Island, is affectionately known as "Old Barney."

Left: Cape May is home to one of the country's largest concentrations of beautiful Victorian structures, like the Abbey, a bed and breakfast inn.

Above: A display of ribbons in one of the atmospheric common rooms in the Abbey.

Right: A re-enactor brings Dr. Emlen Physick to life at the Physick Estate in Cape May. Run by the Mid-Atlantic Center for the Arts, the Physick Estate is the only Victorian house museum in New Jersey. Tours of the estate and the nearby tearoom are open to the public.

🌿 *Left and above:* Renovating an 1872 building, Tom and Sue Carroll opened the elegant Mainstay Inn in 1971 as Cape May's first bed and breakfast inn. They were recently recognized as the senior B&B innkeepers in the country. Don't miss the elegant afternoon tea.

The historic Chalfonte Hotel was built in 1876 by Colonel Henry Sawyer and originally served as a boarding house.

🍁 *Above:* A little girl befriends a kitten on the steps of one of Cape May's Victorian mansions.

🍁 *Right:* Flowers decorate the railings of a vintage home in Ocean Grove.

❧ *Left:* The exotic themes, wacky signs and jutting rooflines of Wildwood's 50's era motels have earned Wildwood the monicker of the home of "Doo Wop" architecture. The Doo Wop Preservation League, which operates this small museum in the heart of Wildwood, is a non-profit organization whose mission is to preserve the fast vanishing style of architecture.

❧ *Above and right:* Two of the funky neon signs from Wildwood's wide selection of Doo Wop-era motels.

🍂 *Left:* Many of the Jersey Shore's most interesting architectural follies had their roots in commercial enterprises. Lucy, the Margate Elephant, was created by real estate salesman James Vincent de Paul Lafferty Jr., who built the four-story structure in 1881 to attract buyers to the then-worthless beachfront properties south of Atlantic City.

Over the years, the 65-foot-tall pachyderm has served as a summer home, a tavern, and a tourist attraction. Wearing away and facing destruction, the structure was saved thanks to the efforts of the Save Lucy Committee, which moved and began restoring her in 1970. In 1976, Lucy was recognized on the National Register of Historic Places.

Upper left and above: A $3 million renovation restored the Starlux to its Doo Wop splendor.

✿ *Above:* Legend has it that saltwater taffy got its name after a summer storm soaked the taffy supply of a candy vendor in Atlantic City in 1888. Joseph Fralinger popularized it and became Atlantic City's first Saltwater Taffy King. Today, the company uses packaging that features vintage artwork.

✿ *Left:* At Shriver's in Ocean City, saltwater taffy is still pulled the old-fashioned way. Although at one point there were over 450 companies producing the candy, today it is in the hands of a few family-run operations like Shriver's, Fralinger's, and James'.

✿ *Right:* Satisfying the seaside sweet tooth is the specialty of ice cream parlors up and down the shore, like Nagle's in Ocean Grove.

🔥 *Left:* The town of Ocean Grove was founded in 1869 as a summer camp meeting retreat by the Methodist Church. The Great Auditorium, built in 1894, serves as the centerpiece of the camp and can hold up to 7,000 people. Besides Sunday services, it hosts concerts and special events.

🔥 *Right:* Over 100 tents surround the Auditorium and the families who summer there are often the fourth or even fifth generation to do so.

🔥 *Above:* A statue of Elwood Stokes, one of Ocean Grove's first spiritual leaders, sits outside the Great Auditorium.

Left: Master craftsman W. Fred Reitmeyer, Jr. carves a decoy in one of the workshops at Tuckerton Seaport, a restored village that highlights the heritage and traditions of the southern Jersey Shore.

Right: A closeup of a decoy at one of Tuckerton Village's two decoy carving shops.

Below: This replica of the Tucker's Island light-house stands at the heart of the restored village. The original was washed away in a ferocious storm in 1927.

The Bays & Beyond

At some points along the Jersey coast, only a few hundred yards separate the ocean from the bays. Nevertheless, they are worlds apart. While the oceanfront may belong to beach-loving vacationers, the bays are the provenance of fisherman, hikers, bird watchers, and hunters; many of whom call the Shore their home. Here, speed boats share the serpentine waterways with sneakboxes—low slung wooden hunting boats unique to these waters and usually handmade by local craftsman.

Here too begins the 1.1-million-acre Pinelands National Reserve, the country's first National Reserve and the largest wilderness area on the East Coast between Boston and Richmond. The Pine Barrens, as they are known, range from northern Ocean County south and west, and occupy 22% of New Jersey's land area. The aquifer beneath them holds some 17 trillion gallons of fresh, pure water.

Besides offering unique natural beauty and an astonishing array of flora and fauna, the Pine Barrens have fostered many legends. The famous Jersey Devil, a fabled creature that first "appeared" here in 1735, has been spotted hundreds of times over the ensuing years, including by naval war hero Stephen Decatur, who claimed to have fired a cannonball through it to no effect.

One eyewitness in 1909 described it as "about three feet and half high, with a head like a collie dog and a face like a horse. It had a long neck, wings about two feet long, and its back legs were like those of a crane, and it had horse's hooves. It walked on its back legs and held up two short front legs..."

It's a vision that has kept many a Pine Barrens camper up at night and definitely something to keep an eye out for on long drives back from the Jersey Shore!

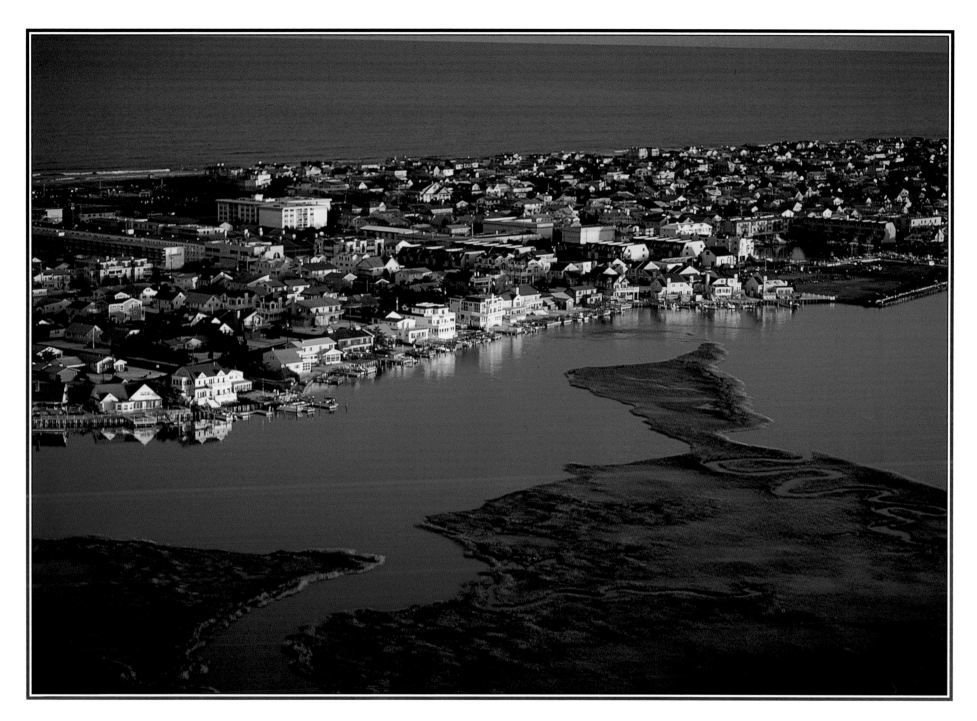

The light of the setting sun bathes bayside houses in a golden glow.

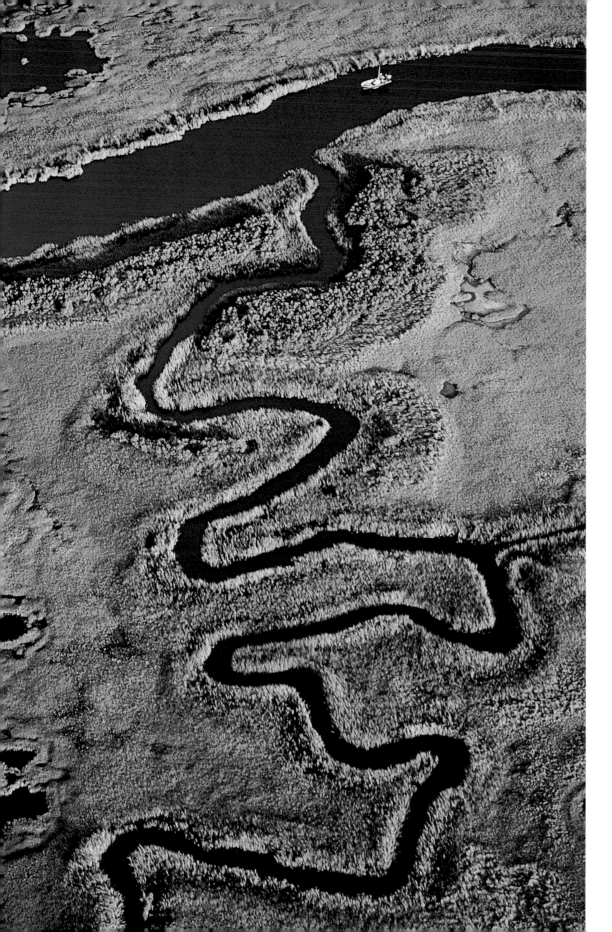

Left: A speedboat navigates the serpentine canals through the marshes of Little Egg Harbor.

Above: Houses line the bay shore near Wildwood.

Right: The bays of the Jersey Shore bridge the gap between the beaches and the vast Pine Barrens.

Left: Thousands of shorebirds flock to Reeds Beach in Cape May at springtime.   *Above:* Herons in a rookery in a park in Avalon.

🐟 *Far left and above:* Canoeists and river grass in the cedar-rich waters of the Batsto River.

🐟 *Right:* Known as "The Tracker," author and back-woodsman Tom Brown (in gray sweatshirt) teaches survival and camouflage skills at workshops deep in the Pine Barrens.

🐟 *Following pages:* Historic Batsto Village was once an iron-making center.

Legendary "Piney" Sam Hunt, a master boat and furniture builder, plays harmonica and banjo in the Pineconers band

Another Pinelands legend and Pineconer, the late Joe Albert, fed wild deer mouth-to-mouth at his home in the woods.

🐟 *Left:* The weekly "Sounds Of The Jersey Pines" show is presented at the Albert Music Hall.

🐟 *Above:* A Jersey Devil tattoo on the calf of one of the musicians warming up for a night of bluegrass music.

Musicians warm up in the adjacent garage, known as the "Pickin Shed," before taking the stage at the Albert Music Hall.

Left and above: There are 3,500 acres cultivated in the Pine Barrens for cranberries, which account for over ten percent of the nation's crop and make New Jersey the country's third-largest producer, behind Massachusetts and Wisconsin. Many farms have been in the same family for generations.

Left and above: The first commercial cultivation of blueberries in the nation happened in the Pine Barrens in 1916, largely to the work of Elizabeth Coleman White, the daughter of a cranberry grower. All of the state's commercial blueberry crops are raised in the Pine Barrens.

🐟 *Above:* New Jersey ranks second in the nation in blueberry production

🐟 *Right:* A leaning tower of empty blueberry boxes is about to rain down on this youngster at a farm near Chatsworth.

The circa 1927 *A.J. Meerwald* was one of hundreds of schooners built along the Delaware Bay shore. Visitors can work the decks of the gaff-rigged oyster dredge, designated as New Jersey's official tall ship in 1998.

CAPTIONS:

 Pages 94–95: Sunset over Barnegat Bay.

 Opposite: The faint red light of pre-dawn and a long camera shutter speed render the waves breaking on Spray Beach as an impressionistic blur.

 Back endpaper: A sunny afternoon on the beach at Seaside Heights.

 Back cover: Night-time action on Morey's Pier in Wildwood.